MALTI

NEESHANT SRIVASTAVA

A gift to people that were born to serve and feel the music of heaven.

Contents

Contents

Preface

'Malti' is a book of poems containing thirty-five poems. 'Malti', incidentally is the name of a common flower found in Eastern parts of India. It is also the name of my Nani (granny). She spent most of her life in Darbhanga, Bihar, where I was born, and was a remarkable lady. The book starts with fond memories of her and the way she guided and managed the affairs of a huge family, strong and defiant, and most of all gave me a beautiful mother.

This book is inclined towards spirituality, as you can tell, a focus of most of my books of poetry. I am no saint or a great leader and I did not hear that word at all from my parents and the rest of the family. I am a simple boy, born in the darkness of a small town of Darbhanga, quite remote to the ways of a bustling city. If I have some insight into spirituality, the credit goes to my parents. If nothing else they were truthful and taught me that a lie is the greatest bane of any life. I tried to speak the truth more or less, as much as I could. It led me to a greater realization that if there is truth on the lips of a person then God shall give him/her a happy and successful life and most of all protect him/her from the shades of evil. My poems are a message to those people that have some innocence in them and are trying to find the path that could lead them to 'samadhi'. It's a very narrow road of fire and pain and I believe that God is sure that we all can reach there in one lifetime, if only we try. For that one has to be truthful to oneself and others.

I have been writing poems for the last ten years on a regular basis. I started out by writing my first poem called 'The Moon' when I was thirteen years old. Life and such matters did not allow me to write on a consistent basis. I returned to my home in Patna and ever since I decided to save the poems I wrote from that point of time. I think my poems make some sense.

1. MALTI

Bush of flowers of common red and white,
They grow together in numerous bunches,
Are the drooping flowers in constant shyness,
Or is it the melancholy of my life so far,
A fragrance too common for the flesh,
Indeed, an emblem for the working class,
An expression of anger for a hasty pluck,
What with lavender, lily, magnolia, jasmine,
It is most uninviting and unfit for a garland,
I saw them in plenty when I was a child,
Growing abundantly on boundary walls,
Of my dear Nani's(granny) home,
Malti, sweet and brave, the voice of a generation,
The light for five children and a soft husband,
Christened 'Malti' after a common man's flower,
She grew up in a mud baked home with roofs of straw,
Lying low in complete respect and awe like those flowers,
Of people that would not peek at her drooping shyness,
Walking the path that drowned those flowers,
Under a constant cloud of rain,
And stole the life out of them,
A lady that left fear and ignorance far behind,
And carved a road that led a family of nothing children,
She looked into my eyes with pride,
A tear perhaps she urged with delight,

'Don't forget, you belong to the land,
Where bushes of Malti grow in plenty'.

2. HAS ANYONE SEEN

• 3 •

Has anyone seen this garden of twilight,
Soft beams of light illuminating the green,
Like He's strolling peacefully in this abode,
A fitting end to the bright scream,
When the mighty owl was blinded and mistaken,
And lost as it accidently hopped out of its home,
Elements of heaven and a chaotic world,
Slamming cars and sirens of catastrophe,
The eyes have sunk too low for a heavenly walk,
The flowers do not speak of colours,
The leaves have hidden the green and abated,
With plasters of dust and trees have sunk,
There is a world far away in Mars,
And the human race has a feather to its cap,
Man in his quest for beauty,
Bag packing to those hills and valleys of green,
Can only flatten the beauty to a city of smoke,
For it's here right now in this silent corner,
A soft meadow of twilight and sleeping green,
A small breath in endless years of existence,
When the journey so far comes to an end,
As we sail away from the constant churn,
Of life and the land of trauma.

3. DIVINE DRILL

Ever heard of a voice when in silence,
It is the voice of heaven,
It does not give clear answers,
To a constant questioning self,
Monday for a question ringing loud,
Is it right to seek that girl I found,
Tuesday still louder,
Are these hands meant for the trade I am in,
Like something forced on the divine,
When the answer always is a forced yes,
Like an unstable mass floating on a lake,
An affirmation to the self, wanting a certain answer,
The voice gives directions in the moment,
Like an army drill when soldiers bend their parts,
In sync to the astute eyes of a commander,
When a sick moment is enough to suffer his wrath,
The divine voice is a guide for a split-second deflection,
Of body parts that mean nothing for the mind,
That is far away in a relentless war with thoughts,
Don't miss the pointed finger to the right,
On the crossroads in an evening walk,
Showing us the safe route home,
Unbelievable but true,
Obey you must to be saved from an avalanche,
When the cruel time comes to make a choice,

Like on that Monday or Tuesday,
For He has a panache for the subtle,
Humbler than the humblest,
Seek Him and you shall never be sad.

4. WHAT MAN ARE YOU

A man with his pure heart,

Is just a man and a man he is,

His actions are as this as air,

His pain a topic of a warm discussion,

His intentions as unreal as stars on a cloudy night sky,

His accomplishments meant for the silent heavens,

His being a sign of evil for an elite corner,

The Maker uncertain of the man that gave of himself,

Stripped and stolen of everything but flesh,

A cost for the pure too dear for the elite,

The world with shut eyes can half see,

For what is a mother to a son after she leaves,

Or a father sleepless for a hundred years,

If there is no heaven then are we just slaves,

With our souls like emptiness of ages,

A pure man should never return,

To a land with no sun or moon,

Where existence has lost its presence,

And the nights have no music or bliss,

Hurry up Stranger for he can see,

The bright garden lying low,

He can't wait for the land of untouched glory.

5. MAGNUM OPUS

Two young ones tied in marriage,

He says it's the end of the road,

His art hidden and lost in search of bread,

Two children and a pile on his table,

Life left no room for freedom and evolution,

Life and times of a writer that he never could be,

A scribbled line somewhere and no sign of a peak,

Anger spilled like tea off an elusive cup in hand,

Twenty-one years and not a book read,

The only hope left were two boys,

That were far from being fertile seeds,

Such idiots would end up as blisters on Mother earth,

Why then does a man have children,

Why is it wrong for a father to hope,

That his children go beyond his own efforts,

And be great examples to the world,

Of unseen courage to the extent of the rarest flight,

For to a son this opportunity has been given,

His love was a hot blade of wrath and ardent slaps,

A kick off the foot and some more hands,

A method of insanity sure to make him the cruel one,

An unpopular man with trembling hands,

He pushed the two into a hot flame of an uncouth world,

A place of hyenas and bloody vultures and no hygiene,

Death and disease in the water and air,

While he too suffered the onslaught,

Lurking around his death bed as the scum grew,

He was gone before any signs,

Of his magnum opus that is so rare,

A magnificent tree emerged to give shade to the world,

So strong and powerful beyond the old man's dream,

A flight that astonished him as he sat somewhere watching,

A tear in proud eyes, he's forcing the day ahead with greater plans.

6. O! RIVER

O! River when did you part,

Into a stream so alone,

That has dried into rocks and died,

Was it your current that the stream couldn't bear,

A sweet child of tomorrow and mother's eyes,

Calm and unmoved by tragedy,

Enough to pull mighty tributaries to itself,

It was the river once in the melting ice,

Destined for the ocean, the end and the beginning,

Why then did it go far away,

Never to even think of a reunion,

What words were exchanged, what was said,

On that fatal night when the river was soft as a mirror,

What made you so silent and swallow yourself,

To carry such oceans of great currents within you,

And not seek a heart to pour your venom that you carry,

Was the magnitude of such too much to imagine,

Was it indeed too late, my friend,

I would say you are the holiest of all,

But now we must measure the damage,

Why did you ever think of holding your steps,

Five years and you did not utter a word,

And formed a patch of dead river,

You spoke to little, when you did,

Become the ocean if you can,

When God pushes you again from your origin,
You are not this stream, you never were.

7. THOSE SMOKED HALLS

Those smoked halls have walls of black,
Where the sun never rises and the moon is gone,
Where no one ever comes and eyes are of stone,
Watching the black rain in an illusion of colours,
Constant and spilling the usual beans of the human race,
They're still engaged in swatting paltry gains with subtle deception,
While casting a delusion that they are what they appear to be,
This humanity bends and bends low only for a jiffy,
As the world leaves them in parts to those lonely smoked halls,
Evening and they wait for eyes to draw its black curtain,
And they be lost in another world of blackened skies,
When did you try to find an easy way by to raise a fortune,
By stealing someone's land and cheating them by your guile,
Given they were people of good heart and easy to deceive,
For one day, and it shall arrive, you will pay dearly,
For no one can hide behind those smoked halls,
Every dark night is born again as a bright day,
When evil doers face the worst plight known to man,
Look your own acts have stolen your hands,
You are but the black of the gutters that swim,
Those smoked halls are below His imagination,
They will not change except for some more soot,
Until the time comes for the great drama,
Our times have just begun to look bad.

8. TOO MANY DEATHS

What is the worth of a human life,

So many lives have ended too soon,

To guns and swords in wars of hatred,

In battles with an indifferent and spiteful world,

Lives not lived until the glorious moon of freedom,

Too many people blown away like dust in a storm,

If it's a heavenly plan then it is quite unfair,

The road to life is the most difficult they say,

Perhaps the way out is an attempt to free oneself,

Who has seen that road as thin as a hair strand,

When the one on it is guaranteed a complete life,

And the tree fully grown to its last summit,

Has always been that mama without a past,

The cliché perhaps shines that it is a journey,

And the fall is a chain to stumble on that glorious moon,

There are those that cannot be free in a hundred,

Like they have heard of the imminent interlude,

Stalling their end with continuous rejuvenation,

Nature and fate call for the person within,

For every human must shine as themselves,

And put an end to guns and swords and sworn hatred,

To carry some weight and not act as deluded young,

For the river is deep but we are human enough,

To quietly sail to the other end.

9. HELP US

We have walked high and low,
Through sweat and blood and the heavy load,
O! Man of hearts please set us free,
Can you walk on embers that glow,
Can you promise to hold that walk,
For ages, bereft of the human longings,
Are you enough to bear the cost, O! Son,
Do not feel the injustice or the hurt along the way,
For we are guilty too,
O! Man, we cry for your insanity,
And we don't know why He did so,
A promise you made should never be broken,
May God take everything away from you,
Don't think, just dive, it's been too long and dark,
We cry for mercy, my son,
We are too old to even hope for something,
We have walked right but never reached the very end,
Were we not enough, my lad,
It's the final hour and we cannot hold our eyes,
We love you and know that you will,
For there was no one with a heart like yours.

10. WHAT NOW, MY SON

I brought you here my son,

I was quiet and pensive as you grew,

Hoping that you remain unaware of this world,

I cannot tell you why for I did not win the battle completely,

Your mind is your greatest enemy, my boy,

You cannot survive in a crowd of motley intruders,

Each one boasting higher than the other,

As you try to kill them with your paltry heritage,

You will lie, and deceive and fill up this vicious hot air balloon,

You will not believe me when I say,

That your common gear, unheard and unsung,

Is your greatest treasure and that there is a Divine force,

You are too weak to handle the crowds of ages,

You are but a slave to their eyes and that is the fatale finale,

Don't try to open your eyes, my son,

You have to give a heavy cost,

You don't know how and when,

The Divine could catch up with you,

Don't try to figure out a way,

By say a cataclysmic insanity,

Your end was defined before your intention,

See all of humanity including me,

Falling through that free fall water slide,

Can we ever see the light after some great battle,

What now, my son!

11. I AM NOT LONELY

How did I happen to reach you, O! Love,

That slight of footprints has gone,

I am a case of emergency hospital with no cost,

My obituary is out and I am the floor,

Of an audacious tent on bamboos,

My saviour sounded that bugle years ago,

And pushed an impossible strain of green in me,

'You can be alone but never lonely, my son',

'For His eyes have merged into yours',

It's hard to explain even to myself of the truth,

I am a sweet gazer of the death of me,

I have company though, of the infinite,

Like a song that is best heard in silence,

I look blankly at the soft waves of this sweet river,

Hoping for a word as I melt into a beautiful moment,

My being an offshoot of mayhem and chaos,

Cannot sometimes bear the heavy weather of total peace,

Sit with me, like a lover that invites me into this world of hush,

When I forgot my life thus,

Take me away, O! lover, I have begun to feel,

A place that is quite enough and more,

For I am not lonely at all.

12. THE DEPTH OF ART

Artists in a flight above the clouds,
As humans a witness to the throbbing world,
With opened eyes that took ages to unfold,
Messages from afar,
From the human minds that held their vision,
Somone seated on the boughs with swinging legs,
Utters in clarity as the artist pictures it perfectly,
A world that will not say a thing,
Yet the artist fully absorbs the moment,
The straight river, full and thick with words,
That clearly shows the beautiful mind and heart,
Possessed by the whispers of a doting Mother,
Pleading with the lost façade,
'You are a good man',
'And so, you shall reap to the depth of the soil',
'You are into the roots of this land',
'And you shall prosper in a world never seen',
'High above the clouds of the clouds',
'For you have earned these moments of silent bliss',
'Be patient, this time no one can hear you',
'And no one shall steal from you',
'Look at me babe, you are in safe hands',
'Carry Me to the depths of your aching heart',
'And reveal a word that is new and exciting',
'Something that I have never heard from anyone',

'For I want to vent this sorrow burning within'.

13. MARRED BY ILLUSION

Why do we have to start new,
And learn to swim in this great ocean,
A game that is quite simple,
Enter the seducer and plenty of lean fish,
Swarming in the starry dazzle trying their luck,
Plenty of love here,
Like those eyes could die for me,
When no one is prepared to budge an inch for others,
Do not despair, there are ways to that palace of dreams,
We have time and a life to strategize,
To hold the greatest dome in time,
To be the greatest living soul ever conceived,
Like the world falling like pins before us as a domino,
Someone is filling up my mind with images,
Of the sought after life leading to prosperity,
Like a novice I give in and almost manage,
To catch the corner of the depleting end of dazzle,
We are all marred by illusion,
And there is no way out,
Ask the man who had it all,
And he shall project an empty life on his death bed,
A life that was never peaceful,
Not for one moment did he sit alone with himself,
And enjoy his hours with an empty mind,

Not for one drop of time was he rich,

Freedom is a costly thing,

And the fishes shall ever delight the ocean.

• 19 •

14. FLOWERS WITH THORNS

Shami my humble offer to thee, Lord Shiva,
My first glimpse of the divine,
Proud in my abode, made of soft wood,
A tree as old as the youth of my parents,
Scanty and forlorn I never saw flowers on it,
A prayer of Lord Ram after a battle of crucifixion,
Pandavas in Mahabharata concealed their weapons in your breast,
Many years and many miles and I, a rock of green,
My feet sore after years of pushing them for nonchalant fingers,
Pointing to my sudden death and more,
Wonder why and how I do not fly by the city any more,
And stay cooped up in my small room even for the rains,
I happened to stop at a car service with blue strong men,
Who spent their days in revolving spanners and tough wrench,
Moving the wheels of a progressive country,
Much to my surprise there was a shami tree,
With flowers that never existed,
With a beautiful array of yellow and pink spikes,
That did not prick but curved under the heat,
Like a beautiful maiden with pink cheeks and yellow dress,
That curved in shyness when accosted by a lover,
One meant for each hardworking man that never loved,
Why then my house had no glitter of flowers,
On the frail shami tree with soft wood that could be scooped out,

O! Sire of old, I wish to see a trace of my beloved,

With pink cheeks and a yellow dress,

For I have never loved.

15. THE FINAL REST

They say no one ever did finally rest,
Lots of names of people buried in history,
Gurus and their methods saving millions of incarnations,
Saying, that is the right way to conquer the invisible sacred,
Just one lifetime is too brief for the perfect 'sadhana',
Like the Divine is a hustle down the tested lane,
And He does not belong to the struggling rest,
Like there is no value of truth or purity of love,
And no ordinary man can yearn for the Holy,
A life in the living present and not in dark caves of the hills,
A life in the bustling city surrounded by a deafening circus,
An ordinary life with the mind in a ceaseless mess,
Can no one from among them without the saffron or shaven head,
Is the Almighty a roadmap, a detour, a bypass,
This is a pledge for all those brave women and men,
That laid down their lives for others,
Without longing for saffron or a mention in history,
With a pure love that was too hard to believe,
That suffered the world but did not stop or change with seasons,
And did find a place in the books of the final judgement,
As a great and a sweet soul and so be rewarded aptly,
He is watching all of us and He belongs to such brave people,
That lived in a corner far away from the world, unsung, unheard,
They are the softness in this world,
And He is preparing their final rest.

16. ANGEL OF BLUE

A child is born and the angel whispers,
What is it that you want to have, my love,
Fame and money fitting a king or a queen,
This large body of land to carry for a million years,
A rebuttal for those eyes that doubted their flight,
The angel is kind and with sad eyes lends enough,
To everyone that ever wished and wished some more,
Yet a lad in the crowd and almost by accident,
In blood and tears looking within as if he met the angel,
In a land of Gods that ripped his flesh too deep,
He is crying in pain, yet stops at a demanding voice,
Pushing him to correct his actions and reform his ways,
The world is converging to give him a better life,
A complete 'naïve' he sits on the edge of insanity,
The angels in huge numbers all through his youth,
It's an endless battle and he has lost his prudence,
An absurd lad carried by whims of soft and stern voices,
In a sea that will never rest as waves just get bigger,
Where is the blue angel, does anyone know,
He has sworn to stay in silence with shut eyes,
Why suddenly did He wipe the dust off his magic flute,
The lad has been rescued by his own slayers,
He has no hope left as angels engage in serious games,
He is in thick slush and the blue angel is blowing air,
To a flute that throws dust like a yellow stream,

The next moment He is sitting next to the lad,
He reflects shades of blue and violet above and below,
He smiles and stands apart looking into the distance,
He leaves the lad and the sound of the flute lingers,
One lad and a musical land,
To leave all his sorrow and enter the highest space,
Far away from wishes and eyes that hurt.

17. ART AND ARTIST

What is art and what is an artist,

Millions of artists smitten by the fame bug,

An art that will fill the coffers of dented pride,

Is art without a purpose,

Why should the woods be deprived of birds,

Where every bird can push a better sound,

Or an art reminiscent of the past glorious hand,

Is art an invention to stun the heathen crowd,

Are the divine hands just a gift for random strokes,

Is the art an end for the artist to raise bread,

The air is abounded with infinite works of art,

Each attempt unsure of its weight and worth,

It's written on the walls that a handful shall ring for long,

While the rest shall die undone and abrupt,

What then is the motto of art and the divine ink,

An artist has to fulfil heaven's desire,

To lift a soul high enough, safe among the clouds,

Far away from the deadly swamp of a conspiring world,

To snatch the soul from the claws of indefinite insanity,

Thus then has the artist fulfilled his purpose,

And the artist with his consummate art shall live forever,

One person and his art a saviour of one soul,

The artist then shall hear from the heavens,

The soul shall rejoice and lend a hand to the artist himself,

An artist that fulfils the divine plan,

Has served the purpose.

18. FEMININE RAYS

No words can summon the reason why,
God created a feminine shade,
She is the creator of the human race,
Subtle and soft like the last drop of rain after a pour,
More powerful than men could ever be,
Yet with a stark element of submission and vulnerability,
O! Woman of seasons when can I ever know you,
Why do you carry long hair and gullible eyes,
Why is you face bringer of bright mornings,
And crescent cheeks the calmness of a sunset flush,
Where is it that you lead me,
I have learnt to swim on avenging high tides,
With the rattling sound of death on unceasing seas,
While you are nowhere to be found in the scorching clime,
You can elicit a sweet sound from a barren land,
You run deep in the marrow of this impoverished sand,
Heaven resides within you,
While I shall struggle to sink in your wavelength,
Like flying kites that have forsaken the earth,
This world of men has embraced a twisted saga,
For a macho is the end of an unfelt divinity,
Of a saviour of love in the reverberating bangles,
Or in a tinkle of the soft anklet,
A herald of a happy end,
For you remain as elusive as the endless ages,

And a sad requiem for paltry skimmers of hell.

19. ARE YOU BEAUTIFUL

A question each one must ask himself/,

In a world that is thinner than the era before,

A quick fix generation that is more artificial than real,

A snap carrier and a louder scream for a perfect body,

A wasted Mother Earth they don't need food to survive,

Size zero and white flesh makes them the richest around,

Like flies on garbage, they settle on the eye worthy,

Fixing a price to devour the flesh,

They have left that wave that is too high,

Milking the senses for pleasure and ease,

For a life that's easy and sorted too soon,

The river gazes in the distance for valour of old,

That could test its waters and cross it sinking to its bed,

To hear the voice far in the distance that longs for,

The hands of the ferryman that saved those souls,

And drowned and died to remerge once again,

To walk the roads of that grand kingdom,

The most beautiful man God had ever seen,

Don't go any further O! traveller of the world,

There are deep crevices ahead and storms of darkness,

A loss of senses and a mind of animals,

For the flesh shall adorn itself over and over again,

Let the Mother provide us with health and beauty,

Let love be our saviour for the children of God,

Yes, we are all very beautiful and will ever be,
Let's lend a helping hand to humanity,
And fight for every tear in our Brother's eyes,
And He shall lend us endless beauty,
Just like the warm sunrise with flashes of colours.

20. FIND ME IN A ROSE

Find me in a rose you man of the lower senses,

That summer's gone, that season of sauté,

I float around all day on petals of shine,

On silvery grass and hedges of gold,

On satin pink and pearly white,

Clear and total without a speck of thought,

All alone within these four walls of heaven,

While you struggle with faces and evil,

An uninvited guest that will not leave,

That woman who presents herself too often,

To trap you in her snare of beauty and flesh,

Kind as the first touch of cold,

In a long and never-ending season of summer,

Too sure of her body that she shall have you,

Wasted long hours when the angel of silence,

Would rather hold you and caress your broken body,

To take you far away into the land of dreams,

Just you and no mind, only clear oceans of still air,

Rise O! brave hearted why do you stoop in pain,

Just one moment as you enter softly,

And slowly the mighty ocean to steal you away,

Into a world of solitary bliss,

Trying to find survivors and escapers,

Find me once again in a rose, O! mighty friend.

21. MY OLD MAN

My old man died young,
A marriage to a beautiful woman,
Yet the beauty ebbed away very soon,
Leaving two people without a reason for love,
My old man died the day my mother turned into a woman,
He had seen extreme lows and creamy highs,
Like a solemn permission from above to end his life,
A desire of a perfect life of a bachelor was foolish,
Life progressed with the birth of two kids,
A sweet gift of my mother to her man,
Like a divine calling he gave up his shape,
And put on the garb of a struggling man,
His eyes just wanted to see and his hands longed to feel,
The thought of an abrupt end left his gaze,
I could never understand his verve,
For two useless kids that would never make it,
His mood swings would often bring him to his old self,
He saw something in us that was hard to imagine,
My old man never gave up on his children,
With me in the nest for good,
I loved the man meant for the silver screen,
His grace was a gift of God,
My hero, my idol, and me a mesmerized fool,
A man who sacrificed the very skin he wore,
A man reduced to tatters and a sickening house arrest,

How can someone have such passion for perpetual frogs,

He took his life like a divine calling,

Not a big deal for a man,

That carried his life in his pocket,

Just a matter of the right time,

A man that lived for his children alone,

Yet there's something in this blood,

A shining tribute to a great artist and his work.

22. O! SWEET LORD

A beginning far from a shadow of life,

A childhood and a shroud of dark evil,

Gimpses of laughter and easy weather,

Good Lord suddenly appeared among the clouds,

Give me your childhood if you may,

Like a suffocating child to put up with dark dreams at night,

Like a cup with some content shaken by a spilling hand,

Speak up you rotting earth don't speak of despair,

Like you have been denied the free will of a child,

Dance the season of rain and plunder the pain,

A boy just stepped into his youth,

Tall and slim, far from the usual shape of manhood,

Childhood's gone and so have the demons of night dreams,

Good Lord suddenly appeared among the clouds,

Given me your youth if you may,

Pull me from among the skies, and you can,

I shall give you the master plan,

Open your gates but do not dive into the waters,

Stay away from those mischievous blue eyes,

But please do not deny someone a walk into you,

This is the toughest ask and shall give you poverty,

Ten more years and I have come to warn you,

Give me your youth, my son, you are almost there,

I shall set you free and no one shall touch you,

Look my child, I have won, sit back,

While I wrap you away from the fire,
O! Sweet Lord my life has just begun.

23. THE HORSE AND THE CARRIAGE

The horse with blinkers beaten to death,

To pull a carriage of three,

Past the mountains above the clouds,

Into a world that expectant eyes await,

The carriage emptied as the horse turned around,

For the one that had been left behind,

A painstaking journey and the horse revived,

The horse fed with grass with the blinkers,

A promise made should not be broken,

Carry us strong one, you were born to serve,

Don't carry a fragment of the fatal illusion,

That beats on you from mysterious corners,

They have alluring masks with the evil hidden within,

Look the Lord too urges you to fly past those bitches,

We are very near O! mighty one, please help us,

Don't let us come again O! stallion of ages,

We burn a simple fire for you in the cold draught,

We are not the kings that hold immeasurable wealth,

While you have seen the poverty that no one ever has,

Yet we are the chosen ones that the Lord has touched,

The line of beggars begging for centuries,

See the doors close on us from all ends,

While you remain aloof from those straight jabs,

Letting them feast on a soft victory,

Look as you emerge with fire in your eyes,
Spread the blanket of warmth on us tonight,
Let us close our eyes in prayer,
Take us far away O! fortuitous one,
The charioteer has lost his whip.

24. MAGIC SINK

An artist's work changes with every season,
What a man or a woman of thirteen,
A work is a work and carries meaning,
Oft the artist is lost in the chaos of youth,
Behind the force of physical and unheard metaphysical,
When the work shall hide behind veils of naught,
A game of patience and guts of the explorer,
When the sudden illusion can call for a catastrophe,
Don't silence the voice or abandon the plan altogether,
The heart is on low, very low, like a pulse of sunlight,
On a sky heavily covered by clouds and has a low heartbeat,
The steps want to wander and plunder a new horizon,
That seems bright and lively with a helluva crowd under it,
Carry on for God is planning the magic sink,
When yesterday had shades of the callous youth,
Perhaps starting again from the outlines of thirteen,
Today there's a new voice from someone quite unknown,
Let it form gradually and the sink to a brighter sun,
This is the real youth of the mind like a constant flame,
That's bright and jubilant with a greater spirit,
You have now entered a phase of creative perfection,
With art carrying a weight that oft brings tears in silence,
It's God's plan and He probably carried the idea for ages,
Only to see its fruition and suffuse with urgency for the next step,
Come O! artist, a timeless touch of grace,

With a voice that's higher than the mountains.

25. GOLD

Life's greatest mystery is a pot/s of gold,

If in plenty, life takes a rest,

There are no wars to speak of,

An old beggar found a pot of gold,

He transformed into the richest of the richest,

Life was smooth as cream of milk,

Choicest women followed by many children,

No worries or hassles to speak of,

Love was easy as in the eyes of his women,

He had been a beggar all his life,

No skill, no work ever done,

Adept with empty hands, he was,

One day he was left with a dime in his pocket,

All women left and so did the children,

Stealing all his money and leaving him a pair of shoes,

He was back again to begging ways,

Another man died many times for many decades,

A man with worthy hands that could turn the wheels of life,

Rescued, redeemed, God lent him oceans of gold,

Just one dip of hands in it,

And he was in heaven of song and beauty,

Never did he yearn for anything in life again,

A small space and a quiet saunter,

Into the depths of total peace,

Ready to be taken away whenever He wished,

Opening his eyes after the sweet sound of each sleep,
To find the gold glistening like a different land,
And God filled his life with what he had missed,
In the mindless lull and seasons of total darkness.

26. SKIES OF FEAR

Look at your skies O! man of resolve,
The blue is blurred and all is white,
The sun's rays are oblique and dull,
You dismiss the roof and gather your thoughts,
A hasty step forward and a constant frown,
Like a load on your shoulders and a restless bid,
The biting weather like an inauspicious act,
Those drums of valour and daunting grunt,
Will not pacify the skies of apocalyptic white,
As you weather the hanging moment of sapping heart,
Like entangled chains that will not dislodge,
A sudden spark will not deliver the human,
A mighty shake shall harm the near ones and more,
A trace backwards shall not yield the reason,
For the sky of white that carries no water,
Is it too late perhaps the sunken leaves,
That are no more a part of the tree,
Old, crisp, carrying boats of veins,
As they only slither in the storm,
Waiting for the final crush from harmless steps,
And a wish to marry the green again,
And behold fantastical blue skies.

27. GOD'S PARADISE

Have you seen God's paradise,
A land of calm and great beauty,
It's tipping off people that made the grade,
In a solemn prayer to the Almighty,
Dear Lord, take away everything I have,
My possessions, my respect, my reputation,
Strip me off the clothes I wear,
Take away the food on my plate,
Take away the sleep in my eyes,
Let my shoes be torn and my body ache,
Let me fill the shoes of insanity,
And roam around the streets like mendicants,
Or be justified behind the bars of an asylum,
Let them take me and banish to the jungles,
Let me hear the words of truth and die in vain,
A fool that I am, I shall never know an end,
But please lend me a glimpse of the paradise,
After the shapeless body is denied of life,
And I shall never walk the streets again,
I shall close my eyes and be grateful,
To your generous heart,
For showing a life torn and lost,
When evil had won over this timid soil,
A glimpse of the greatest paradise ever known,
Making this life worth living.

28. THE GREATEST ART

The greatest art is not hidden in a painting,
A piece of music, film of actors, poetry, song,
It begins with a blank canvas handed over by the Almighty,
And colours, paint brushes, paraphernalia, and four hands,
The artist at work does not have a glimpse or image in mind,
When he is asked to create himself,
A creation with no knowledge or an advancing path,
A bizarre creation when he is left alone,
For twenty-nine seasons of summer or spring,
A hard road to travel when a little shift of focus,
Shall destroy the creation forever and the artist,
Takes home an unfinished work drowned in lakes of inebriation,
A tight rope walk, a nudge from the cliff is imminent,
The summit is the highest and most beautiful,
A creation by working on formless and imaginary,
And walking a road that does not exist,
Until finally the artist lends final touches, in disbelief,
To the most brilliant creation ever made by human hands,
A creation of the self without those stubborn and dark walls,
That has blinded all artists with a spurious heart,
That longs for patches of beauty and carnival of colours,
That blind the eye looking for symmetric perfection,
In the outside world,
Whilst the real creation is shapeless and formless,
Lying within each human when the self-subsides,

In the rigors behind the most beautiful art ever created,
Take a lifetime and feel the unlimited,
Land on ether and upset the fetters,
That dark night shall ever be forgotten.

29. WHERE IS HEAVEN

A million years and more of civilization,
In search of heaven,
A child finds heaven in the eyes of parents,
Often destroyed by storms at home,
A young man seeks heaven in a soft feminine,
A poor man seeks heaven in far off riches,
A black man seeks heaven in oceans of white,
A lonely man seeks heaven in warmth of intimacy,
A man of dreams seeks heaven in crowds of fame,
A competitor seeks heaven in conquering challenges,
A man of malice seeks heaven in stabbing his neighbour,
A man of career seeks heaven in amassing the world,
A conqueror seeks heaven in ruling over the world,
A woman of standing seeks heaven in rich men of wealth,
An artist seeks heaven in the highest magnum opus,
A worthless man seeks heaven in robbing others,
All seek heaven but are caught in a fate of hell,
A spark or a dying flame like a flash of heaven,
Is all they get in their constant efforts towards,
The shining walls of heaven in a squandered life,
Buddha sought heaven in conquering sadness,
Little did he know till he gave up his royalty,
To become a beggar and roam the streets,
When all desire and thought escaped him,
To finally find heaven in all its glory,

A man bestowed with the gift of a heart,
To feel for each human that crossed his path,
Eyes washed by tears when alone,
A heaven is not too far if we should know.

30. WHERE'S SOMEONE

Time has changed with new faces and hearts,
Strange to hear the phrase 'Our times have gone',
The world is sprinkled with youth and shine,
Promises made and a generation of liars,
Spilled too soon without a passing thought,
That life means patience and curb,
Those darting eyes are looking for someone,
Perhaps an angel and the same desire,
That irked a nation of young long ago,
Those eyes are still looking for someone,
Perhaps a Buddha or Swami Vivekananda,
A spectator to the trails left by people of substance,
Here's a sincere urge to the youth of today,
Look within and set about a chain of reform,
Let that lord be your master and admit shortcomings,
Even if the mind and its mindlessness shall point a finger,
Leave the devil behind and hear the truth,
Remember God has unique ways to talk to you,
Sometimes he adorns the lips of the devil,
That utters words which surprisingly make sense,
And rushes you to do something that you must,
Taking you sometimes to cranky roads,
Exhibit your deviant robe without feeling obscure,
Remember, children, this is your only chance,
Leap over this eccentric and hurtful world,

Let no one ever trap you and milk you,
One small step can fully awaken the Almighty,
If it takes tough so be it,
Come home young soldier,
Be honest and brave in all innocence,
It's a long way home but never taken.

31. WE ARE FAMILY

Don't smash your bones it hurts,
Life is a logic that leads to a valid construction,
Be well dressed and charming and utter what's right,
In a forty year walk to and fro from home to there,
I was the favoured guinea pig,
They had harnessed me to a cart,
Whipped me hard to my very end,
And just in time revived me until the next assault,
Those blinkers did not allow me to see what was happening,
As I died and died but never really died,
I lived on air and my body needed no food,
I came out and wore the crown of insane,
The first and last in the family of four,
I survived on pills and that melancholy song,
They fed me with milk and ghee,
'My boy eats like a glutton; he's been without food...'
That horse's up again, and with a vengeance,
My harness turned me left and right and I obeyed,
I ran and ran in a noisy and distracted world,
Where nobody has any clue where they're headed,
My masters left me and headed towards the sky,
And I still awaited the next snap of fingers,
I didn't know where I was or where I was going,
My insanity was news and I was without pills,
Bonker hours perspiring and using my reserves,

After a half a century I finally died but heard a voice,
They said it was the birth of someone new,
And miles had still dressed before me,
Urging me to run the final lap,
I was saved over and over again,
By three angels,
Bless them Lord for I owe,
This bright new morning peeking at my window.

32. MY SAVIOUR

It is true O! Lord that many don't believe,
The greatest saviour is dismissed and lives carved,
In a long list of complaints and the sin of pain inflicted,
No one can throw away the hatred of life's enemies,
Wanting to vent the anger and be calm as ice once again,
Why to believe in something heard not seen,
For if He's there then where is He,
Life ended long ago and they still have hope,
Of cherished dreams,
They carry the confidence of a saint,
As if the path was their script and their idea,
And life is whatever they want, a wish easily done,
They carry a long history of success,
As if failure is for the foolish and not for wise,
A sudden calamity and their fear is larger than life,
Destroying their very being to shreds,
No one knows when the lightning strikes,
Someone in the crowd says it's God's will,
And silent bearing and perseverance is the way out,
Did anyone call out His name ever,
Like a dying man's wish for help and redemption,
Like a piece of hope for the soul within each of us,
Did anyone cry for eyes that cannot see,
Did anyone cry out for life and not death,
Is anyone willing to suffer the aftermath of truth,

He is sitting among us, like He always has,
And we cannot see,
Save me Lord, I am an epitome of sin,
And through charred hollows of sin I shall rise,
To meet You with my eyes.

33. WIND VANE

Those silent blades of the mighty wind vane,

Silent by the sudden rush of a new age,

Where the winds don't run high with meaning,

And the weather without notice has turned cold,

It will take a gush of breeze to set them alive,

Those new hills of glass and stone disturb the horizon,

An easy prey to the low winds of disaster,

Look their tops are sick in a bout of dizziness,

The wind vanes have grasped the age in subtle shifts,

Those eyes that pierce its flesh need no flagging reminders,

And the wind vane obeys carrying a heavy load of dust,

There was a time when those skilled hands pushed the mighty tower,

Deep into Mother earth with three sparkling blades,

And the sudden gush of breeze set the city aglow,

With the blades in a rush of circles like a promise,

Much like life that must move forward endlessly,

Until God ponders on the path thus covered,

Don't steal that path behind windows of junk,

Take a walk today with eyes that meet the wind,

With the branches of green in whamming steps of grace,

To the lord of song, the gritty breeze,

The same breeze that ages ago shattered the wind vane,

And reached a stunning height of ecstasy,

Starting out patiently from the hems of salty eyebrows,

Of men and woman that ripped their wear with mud and dust,

And lost their faces and bodies to a herculean task,
Of love and truth and life of great sacrifice,
To be of service to others and lend a hand to humanity,
In the creation of the huge wand of love,
The majestic wind wane much like the cross.
*Facts modified for poetic justice

34. THAT TOWN OF HEARTS

That town of hearts has left me dry,

It's not a prayer that I shall end,

And leave this town of sorrow,

Kindness and a heart were a regular in that town,

Elders were soft and oft buried deep and low,

Bright children could feel their hearts,

As the father peeped into his son's eyes,

Like a soft caress and a smile of the heart,

There are places to go and it is not in us to decide,

The final bugle when all must cease,

But good leads to good and so it will be,

The days were bright then and work to be done,

For an unceasing effort was God's design,

The perpetual lag in the mind for us to grow,

And be stronger and better until we realize,

Things that have to wait for long to ring a bell,

Why father believed in his son,

And mother stole him away from the world,

For us to survive long after both have left,

With that wonderful town of hearts,

And lend a meaningful hand to God's end,

I am happy today in a new life,

I belong to the sun and the moon,

And the bouncing beauty of lush trees,

In a mischievous breeze that wants more,
That town of hearts has led to a greater city,
Beyond all expectations and belief,
Me and God above,
I can't wait to rise even higher,
In a tete-a-tete with my folks.

35. WOMAN

She's a woman and she let it be,
I'm looking at her through the eyes of ages,
And I don't like what I see,
Stay away, don't touch, get away,
A voice cried out in the silence,
From a rose that's high and soft,
An easy prey to the beastly hands,
She is higher than men will ever be,
Carrying the feathers of esoteric, abstruse,
For art probably originated from women,
While men could grasp only through eyes and touch,
Woman! What do you see in colour and shapes,
And the dress of linen with embroidered flowers,
Or the baby's sweater with a simple touch of design,
Those homes are museums of artistry,
That speak louder than all words put together,
What a dive into intricate and subtle air of magic,
That's more to decipher than a glaring piece of metal,
How then do you play the jester,
Like an upper chamber that's empty,
To appear like a fool to the pounding men,
O! Woman please, walk that road to the tee,
For a woman is a gift of God,
That has shown the way to a rugged world,
Lending a chance to breathe in the mess around us,

Driving some sense into existence,
Taking us higher in a journey to heaven,
Woman, the creator of humankind,
And the sad story continues.

* 9 7 9 8 8 9 1 3 3 5 5 6 1 *